Thean
Psalter

Thean Psalter
by M. Kate Allen

Thea Press
P.O. Box 24905
Tempe, AZ 85282
www.theapress.org

For more information about M. Kate Allen, see www.lifeloveliturgy.com

First printing, December 2018
ISBN-13: 978-1-7335064-0-3 (Paperback)
ISBN-10: 1-7335064-0-3 (Paperback)

Thean Psalter

~ M. Kate Allen ~

First Day: Morning Prayer

Psalm 1

Happy are they whose delight is in the wisdom of Thea,
   who meditate on her wisdom day and night.

They are like trees planted by streams of water,
   bearing fruit in due season, with leaves that do not wither.

For Thea embraces all among her,
   and touches them with her love.

Psalm 2

Thea said, "You are my daughter;
   this day I have birthed you."

And now, you rulers, be wise;
   be thoughtful, you leaders of creation.

Stand in Thea's midst with awe,
   and with reverence bow in her holy presence.

Psalm 3

You, O Thea, give courage to my heart;
   you lift up my voice.

I call out to you with my voice, O Thea,
   and you answer me from the midst of creation,
   your Sacred Body;

I lie down and go to sleep;
   I wake again, sustained in you.

Psalm 4

I revere you in the morning and in the night, O Thea;
  I speak to my heart in faintest whispers upon my bed.
  Gift me with the warming light of your face, O Thea.

You put gladness in my heart,
  more than when grain and vines and oil increase.

I lie down in peace; I fall asleep at once;
  for you, O Thea, are my safe dwelling.

Psalm 5

Give ear to my words, O Thea;
  consider my meditation.

In the morning, O Thea, you hear my voice;
  early in the morning I whisper and sing to you.

Lead me, O Thea;
  make your ways clear before me.

Transform and heal my errors and wrongdoing,
  for I have wittingly and unwittingly
  rebelled against your wisdom.

Enveloped in you, I will be glad;
  I will sing out my joy forever.

For you, O Thea, will bless me and all creation with peace;
  you will empower your Sacred Body to create again.

First Day: Evening Prayer

Psalm 6

Take care with me, O Thea, for I am trembling;
  heal me, O Thea, for my bones are racked.

My flesh shakes with terror;
　　how long, O Thea, how long?

I grow weary with distress;
　　every night I drench my bed
　　and flood my pillow with tears.

My eyes are wasted with grief
　　and worn away because of this oppression.

Let that which weighs heavily upon me be transformed,
　　for you hear the sound of my weeping, O Thea.

Psalm 7

O Thea, I take refuge in you;
　　deliver me from all who persecute me;

Lest like a lion they tear me in pieces
　　and snatch me away with none to help me.

Let the malice of others come to an end,
　　plant new seeds in their hearts, O Thea.

For you, O Thea, are both clever and loving;
　　and you will break open even the stoniest of hearts.

Psalm 8

O Thea, author of all,
　　how wondrous is your Sacred Body, creation!

From the mouths of infants and children
　　your voice rings out
　　within the valleys and from the peaks,

From all sheep and cattle,
　　even the wild animals that roam,

The birds of the air,
　　the fish and other creatures of the sea.

I ponder your celestial skies, the work of your fingers,
  the moon and the stars in their arrangement.

Who am I that you should be mindful of me?
  who am I but the daughter of so many daughters?

But it is I whom you seek, and you call me by name,
  seeking the beauty of the fire that dwells within me.

With honor and respect,
you offer me knowledge of the works of your hands;
  you put awe of all things within my reach.

O Thea, author of all,
  how wondrous is your Sacred Body, creation!

Second Day: Morning Prayer

Psalm 9

I will bless you, O Thea, with my whole heart;
  I will tell tales of your marvelous works.

I will be glad and rejoice in you;
  I will sing of your heights and your depths, O Thea.

Even now I sing to you whose Sacred Body is creation;
  I sing your wonders amid the wonders you have created.

For you are a haven for those who fear and doubt,
  fertile soil for playful planting.

Strengthen my voice, O Thea,
  so that I may tell of your wonders in all of creation.

Psalm 10

Why do you seem so far off, O Thea,
  hidden in time of trouble?

Those with money boast of their desires;
　　the wealthy curse and revile the poor.

Those who have much care not for others;
　　their first thought is, "My neighbor does not matter."

They lurk in ambush in public squares
and in secret places they attack the unsuspecting;
　　they spy out the helpless.

They lie in wait, like a lion eyeing its prey;
they lie in wait to seize upon the lowly;
　　they seize them and drag them away.

Their victims are broken and humbled before them;
　　they are helpless before their power.

Rise up, O Thea!
　　remember your afflicted ones.

Surely, you behold their trouble and misery;
　　take it into your own hand.

Break the power of those who act unjustly;
　　transform their wickedness until it is no more.

Psalm 11

Thea is holy;
　　Thea's Sacred Body is creation.

Thea beholds her Sacred Body, creation;
　　her discerning eye perceives our interdependence.

Thea protects and uplifts us all,
　　and those who delight in violence she seeks to transform.

For Thea is wise;
　　she delights in wise deeds.

May we come to perceive her in all creation,
　　to experience the unhesitating embrace of her love.

Psalm 12

Help us, O Thea, for there is no wise one left;
  the wise have vanished from among us.

Oh, that you would silence all smooth tongues,
  and close the lips that utter proud boasts!

"Because the needy are oppressed,
and the poor cry out in misery,
  I will rise up," you say,
  "and give them the help they seek."

O Thea, watch over us;
O Thea, empower us;
  help us to find justice when we seek your aid.

Psalm 13

How long, O Thea?
How long shall I be perplexed
  and grieve in my heart, day after day?

Look upon me and answer me, O Thea;
  give light to my eyes, lest I sleep forever.

I put my trust in the strength you offer me;
  my heart is joyful because of your wise help.

I will sing to you, O Thea, for you show me my true self;
  I will praise you with songs of great joy.

Psalm 14

The fool says in her heart,
  "What Thea has created is worthless."

So many commit ruthless, abominable acts;
    where is there one who does any good?

Have they no wisdom, those who do harm,
    who eat up those around them like bread?
    Oh, that creation might be delivered
    from the fingers of malice!

When Thea brings healing
to the wounds of her Sacred Body,
    all creation will rejoice and be glad.

Third Day: Morning Prayer

Psalm 15

O Thea, who is an icon of you?
    Who reveals your Sacred Body?

Each of us—whether blameless or guilty,
    whether she speaks the truth from her heart or deceives;

Whether there is guile upon her tongue;
whether she offers evil or kindness to her friend;
    whether she heaps generosity
    or contempt upon her neighbor;

Whether she has sworn to do no wrong
    or makes a vow and then takes back her word.

We are, each of us, icons of you,
    because we are your living Body,
    broken, holy, and ever healing.

What a marvel, that you should knit us together in your love,
    sustaining us for love's sake alone.

Blessed be Thea, our author and our sacred self,
    now and forever. Amen.

Psalm 16

Protect me, O Thea, for I take refuge in you;
  I say to you, "You are my muse,
    my inspiration above all other."

O Thea, you are my portion and my cup;
  you uphold my life.

I bless you, for you give me counsel;
  my heart teaches me, night after night.

You journey side by side with me;
  because you are with me, I am secure.

My heart, therefore, is glad;
  I dwell in hope.

For you will not abandon me,
  nor let your beloved one journey alone.

You will show me the path of life, O Thea;
  in your presence is fullness of joy,
    and at your side is wisdom forever.

Psalm 17

Hear my voice, O Thea;
  listen to me when I speak.

Slowly, with difficulty,
I am learning to give no offense with my mouth;
  I listen with care to the words of your lips.

Help me, O Thea;
  weigh my heart, summon me by night,
    melt me down; put me to the test.
As you help me, show me your marvelous loving-kindness,
  O stronghold of those who seek wisdom.

Keep me as the apple of your eye;
  hide me under the shadow of your wings.

When I awaken from this slumber I shall see your face,
  and I shall be filled with gladness,
  beholding your Sacred Body for all you are.

Third Day: Evening Prayer

Psalm 18

I love you, O Thea my strength,
  O Thea my strength and my creative haven.

The breakers of death rolled over me,
  and the torrents of oblivion made me afraid.

The ropes of lifelessness entangled me,
  and the snares of death were set for me.

But when I called out to you in my distress,
  my cry came to your ears.

The earth reeled and rocked;
  the roots of the mountains shook;
  they reeled at your answer.

You parted the thick clouds and came to me
  storming forth in your love.

You set forth and flew;
  you swooped on the wings of the wind.

You wrapped darkness about you;
  you made dark waters and dense clouds your pavilion.

From the brightness of your presence, through the clouds,
  burst hailstones and streaks of fire.

You thundered,
  uttering your voice.

You loosed your arrows and scattered them;
  you hurled thunderbolts and routed them.

The beds of the seas were uncovered,
and the foundations of the world laid bare,
   at your fierce cry, O Thea,
   at the blast of your breath.

You reached out and grasped me,
   drawing me out of the great waters.

You brought me out into an open place;
   you rescued me;
   you delighted in me.

You, O Thea, are my lamp;
   you make my darkness bright.

With you I will break down any enclosure;
   with your help I will scale any wall.

Your way is love;
   you are a comfort and shelter.

You bind me with strength
   and make my way safe.

You make my movements steady as that of a deer
   and help me hold firm in the heights.

You train my hands for tremendous works,
   and my arms for bending even a bow of bronze.

You offer me your shield;
   your hand also sustains me;
   your loving care empowers me.

You support my every movement,
   and my body does not give way.

Blessed are you, my love!
   Mighty and gentle are you, O Thea!

I will sing to you in the midst of creation,
your Sacred Body,
   and I will praise you in your holy presence.

Fourth Day: Morning Prayer

Psalm 19

The heavens declare the wonders of Thea,
  and the skies reveal her handiwork.

One day tells its tale to another,
  and one night imparts memory to another.

Their sound goes out into all lands,
  and their message to the ends of the universe.

The wisdom of Thea revives the flesh;
  the love of Thea does not waver.

Awe of Thea endures through every age;
  Thea's wisdom bears resounding truth.

It is more to be desired than fine gold;
  it is sweeter than honey, even honey in the comb.

By it your beloved is enlightened,
  and in keeping it there is great reward.

I seek your wisdom day and night, O Thea;
  but how often do I yet offend with my words and deeds?
  O Thea, cleanse me from my persistent faults.

Guard me from presumption and wrongdoing;
let my faults not overpower me;
  then I shall be whole and sound.

Let the words of my mouth
and the meditation of my heart be true to you,
  O Thea, my strength and my inspiration.

Psalm 20

May Thea answer you when you call,
  send you help from deep within herself,
  and strengthen you out of creation, her Sacred Body;

May she grant you your heart's deepest desire
   and prosper the plans
   that will give birth to your greatest joy.

Shout for joy in the presence of Thea!
   and may she make possible those desires
   which grow hardy in wisdom's soil.

Psalm 21

I rejoice in your love, O Thea,
   and I exult in your wisdom!

You offer me everlasting felicity;
   I lack nothing in your presence.

Emboldened and encouraged by your loving-kindness,
   I leap toward my dreams.

I trust you, O Thea;
   I know I will not falter, even if I fall.

You fulfill my heart's deepest desire;
   you turn my life's aching longing into ecstasy.

Fourth Day: Evening Prayer

Psalm 22

O Thea, why have you forsaken me?
   and why are you so far from my cry?

O Thea, I cry in the daytime;
   by night as well, but I find no rest.

My foremothers put their trust in you;
   they trusted, and you delivered them.

They cried out to you and were delivered;
   they called on you, and you helped them.

You are she who took me out of the womb,
   and kept me safe upon my mother's breast.

I was in your care from the moment I was born;
   indeed, you were my mother's midwife
   when I was still in the womb.

O Thea, now you are my strong, gentle midwife;
   be not far from me, for birthing pangs overtake me,
   and there is none else to help.

My mouth is dried out like a broken pot;
   my tongue sticks to the roof of my mouth.

Be not far away, O Thea;
   you are my strength;
   hasten to help me.

Save me from the sting of death;
   save the new life that stirs within me.

Bring that which dwells within me to birth
with your wise, saving hands,
   and I shall rejoice at the sight of your new icon,
   my great love.

Psalm 23

O Thea, you and I come together as one body,
   curious, alive, and free in one another.

We make love in lush, green meadows;
   beside flowing waters, I caress you into ecstasy.

You envelop me
   and invite me to explore every part of you.

Even when we journey into uncharted terrain,
I fear nothing, for you are with me;
   your hands and your voice comfort me.

You spread yourself before me;
    all I hunger for is you.

You anoint my head with oil,
    and my cup overflows.

Surely our wild, powerful love
shall arouse our creativity all the rest of our days,
    and we will share sighs in one another's arms forever.

Fifth Day: Morning Prayer

Psalm 24

Creation is Thea;
    the universe and all who dwell therein
    are her Sacred Body.

For it is she who splashes as the seas
    and is the firm earth alongside the great rivers.

Who can enter the valley of Thea?
    Who can enter her presence?

Those whom she loves:
    every creature in creation.

All shall receive the blessing and the great joy
    of the one whose Sacred Body they are.

Psalm 25

To you, O Thea, I lift up my voice;
    my love and my lover, I trust in you.

Show me yourself, O Thea,
    and teach me who you are.

You are mine, the breath of my flesh,
    and I am yours.

You bless your beloved with wisdom
   and willingly reveal yourself.

My eyes look to you with wonder and joy,
   for you are my great love.

Psalm 26

O Thea, your creativity captures my gaze;
   I journey side by side with you.

I move joyfully, singing aloud a song of thanksgiving
   for the wonders I have experienced.

O Thea, I love all creation, your Sacred Body,
   the high and low, the wide and narrow places;
   blessed be your Sacred Body forever!

Fifth Day: Evening Prayer

Psalm 27

Thea is my courage;
   whom or what then shall I fear?

One thing I ask of her;
one thing I seek;
   that I may dwell with her all the days of my life;

To behold her mysterious beauty
   and to seek her in every place.

In days of trouble she keeps me safe,
   holding me close in the shelter of her dwelling.

Therefore I open my heart
   with sounds of great gladness!

I sing as I create a new thing;
   mine is the playful body of Thea.

She speaks in my heart and whispers,
"Seek me in all you meet."
    I seek her, therefore, in every creature.

She shows me myriad ways that lead to her;
    and whispers the way that is mine alone to take.

I see her goodness as my path crosses other paths
    in the dewy web of her creation!

Psalm 28

O Thea, hear the sound of my voice
    even when words escape me.

You are my strength and my courage;
    my heart trusts in you.

Move with me, O Thea;
journey side by side with me,
    till I return to the clay
    to be made a new creation.

Psalm 29

The voice of Thea thunders;
    Thea is upon the mighty waters.

The voice of Thea is a powerful voice;
    hers is a voice of splendor.

The voice of Thea breaks the cedar trees;
    Thea splits the cedars.

The voice of Thea rends the flames of fire;
    the voice of Thea shakes the wilderness.

The voice of Thea makes the oak trees writhe
    and strips the forests bare.

All who hear her
   tremble with awe.

Thea shall show her strength
through creation, her Sacred Body;
   and Thea shall offer her creatures the blessing of peace.

Sixth Day: Morning Prayer

Psalm 30

I weep in your presence, O Thea,
   because you lifted me up.

You brought me up, O Thea, from the dead;
   you restored my life as I was going down to the grave.

You turned my tears into dancing;
   you stripped me of my mourning
   and clothed me with joy.

I shall sing to you all my days, O Thea,
   giving thanks for your unbounded love.

Psalm 31

In you, O Thea, I take refuge;
   let me not be swallowed up by shame.

For you are my rock and my stronghold;
   journey beside me as I move along this difficult path.

Be with me, O Thea, for I am in trouble;
   my throat and my belly ache,
   and my eyes are consumed with sorrow,

Free me from the net that was set for me,
   for your hands are strong and deft.

Into your hands, I commend my body,
   O Thea, Goddess of love.

I will let my heart take courage
   as I wait upon your loving help, O Thea.

Sixth Day: Evening Prayer

Psalm 32

Happy are they whose wrongful deeds are forgiven,
   and whose evildoing is made right.

At one time I held my tongue,
and my bones withered away
   because of my groaning all day long.

The weight of my evildoing
   lay heavy upon me day and night;
   no spring could quench the guilt that parched me.

Then I acknowledged my wrongs
   and sought to make amends for them.

In time, those whom I injured forgave me,
and the weight of my guilt grew less heavy,
   making way for the peace that heals
   both the one wounded and the one who wounds.

You are my hiding place, O Thea;
   you nurse me back to wholeness.

Great are the trials of those who persist in evil deeds;
   but peace stirs in those who rend their hearts.

Psalm 33

Sing praises, all you creatures,
   to the one who weaves us together
   in patterns of love.

Praise Thea with the harp and woodwind;
  start a dance upon the drums.

Sing her a new song;
  sound a fanfare upon the trumpet;
  make music with your instrument!

Thea loves peace and wisdom, art and story;
  her loving-kindness fills the universe;

She looks upon her Sacred Body, creation,
  and beholds her dear ones in love.

She warms our hearts with her fire
  and witnesses our beautiful and devastating works.

Behold, Thea's eyes are set upon her creatures
  as she journeys alongside us all.

Psalm 34

I will bless Thea at all times;
  blessings shall ever be in my mouth.

I will look upon her and be radiant;
  my face will not fall with shame.

Taste and see that Thea is good;
  happy are they who journey in her wisdom!

Seek her face in all you meet,
  for those who behold her lack nothing.

Come, my daughters, and listen to me;
  I will teach you to stoke the fire
  Thea has lit within you.

Who among you loves life
  and desires it to the full?

Turn from evil and love extravagantly;
  seek peace and pursue it with courage.

The eyes of Thea behold her creatures,
  her Sacred Body,
  and her ears open to their voices.

Seventh Day: Morning Prayer

Psalm 35

Wield the power of your art, Thea,
  and reveal to all the truth of what has happened.

Let those who betrayed me
be caught in the net they hid for me;
  let them fall into the pit they dug.

For when they were brought low
I dressed in mourning clothes
  and humbled myself by fasting;

I prayed with my whole heart,
as one would for a friend or a sister;
  I behaved like one who mourns for her mother,
  bowed down and grieving.

But when I met my moment of weakness
when I was in greatest need of their loving support,
  they gathered against me;
  they turned their backs on me.

They put me to the test instead of lifting me up;
  the warm, vocal love they once showed
  turned to chilling, silent disdain.

Awake, arise!
  Join me in my defense, O Thea!

Help me find justice, O Thea,
  so that those motivated by self-interest alone
  may not have the final word.

Let all who participate in oppression
be clothed with dismay and shame,
   until they recognize their wrongdoing
   and seek to make amends.

And let the liberated sing out with joy and be glad;
   rejoicing side by side with you in newfound freedom.

Psalm 36

There is a voice of rebellion in the depths of your creation;
   there is no awe of anything before her eyes.

She flatters herself in her own eyes
   and embraces what is hateful.

The words of her mouth are unkind and destructive;
   she has abandoned acting wisely.

She thinks up clever forms of wickedness upon her bed
   and deems herself justified in all her actions.

And still your love, O Thea, reaches to the oceans,
   and your faithfulness to the clouds.

Your righteousness is like the strong mountains,
your justice like the great deep;
   you free all your creatures from their bonds,
   O Thea, even this one.

How priceless is your love, O my Goddess!
   your creatures take refuge
   under the shadow of your wings.

They feast upon the abundance of your house;
   you give them drink from the river of your delights.

For with you is the well of life,
   and in your light we see light.

Continue your loving-kindness
   and your favor to your creatures whom you cherish.

Teach the proud to journey humbly,
and the hand of the wicked to reach out in peace.

Seventh Day: Evening Prayer

Psalm 37

Take delight in Thea, your author and your muse,
and your heart's deepest desire will flourish.

Commit your way to her and put your trust in her,
and she will journey with you at every step.

She will make the stuff of your imagining
as vibrant as the first light of day
and the next steps of your creative path
as clear as the noonday.

In the depths of darkness, be still before Thea
and wait patiently for her.

Refrain from anger, leave rage alone;
do not fret yourself.

In a little while wastefulness shall fade away;
you shall search it out, but it will manifest no longer.

Instead, the fruit of your imagination shall prosper
and Thea's Sacred Body will breathe deeply
with awe at your handiwork.

Eighth Day: Morning Prayer

Psalm 38

O Thea, I am utterly bowed down and prostrate;
I weep all day long.

My belly is filled with a searing pain;
  there is no health in my body.

I am utterly numb and crushed;
  I cry out, because of the pain that consumes me.

O Thea, you know all my desires,
  and my tears are not hidden from you.

My heart is pounding, my strength has failed me,
  and the brightness of my eyes is nearly gone.

O Thea, do not forsake me;
  be not far from me in my trouble.

I trust, O Thea, that you will hear my voice;
  I trust that you will answer me.

Do not delay, O Thea;
  make haste to help me.

Psalm 39

I said, "I will keep watch over my ways,
  so that I do not offend with my tongue.

I will put a muzzle on my mouth
  even while those who oppress me are in my presence."

So I held my tongue and said nothing;
  I refrained from rash words;
  but my pain became excruciating.

My heart was hot within me;
while I pondered, the heat burst into flame;
  I lashed out with my tongue,
  and the consequences were unbearable.

O Thea, let me know my end
  and the number of my days,
  so that I may know how short my life is.

You have given me a mere handful of days,
  and my lifetime is as nothing compared to yours.

I move about like a shadow
  and in vain I toil.

And now, what is my hope?
  O Thea, my hope is in you.

Take this affliction from me;
free me from my oppressors,
  for I am worn down.

Hear my prayer, O Thea,
and give ear to my cry;
  do not let my tears go unanswered.

For I am but a sojourner with you,
  a wayfarer, as all my foremothers were.

Grant that I may be glad again,
  before I go my way and am no more.

Psalm 40

I waited for you, O Thea;
  suddenly I felt you bend close to me, listening.

You lifted me out of my pit, out of the mire and clay;
  you set me upon a high cliff
  and made my movements became sure once more.

A new song left my mouth then,
  a song of unfettered joy.

Oh, that I might tell of your wisdom's way!
  but it is beyond my power to describe,
  for it is different for each creature, every one of us.

As for me, I have learned that it is enough to say,
  "Behold, I come."

In your book it is written concerning me:
  'I love to do your will, O Thea;
  your wisdom is deep in my heart.'"

Psalm 41

Those who resist prophetic words
  against their selfish deeds ask of me:
  "When will she die, and her name perish?"

Even my dearest friend, whom I trusted,
who broke bread with me,
  lifted up her heel and turned against me.

But I shall rise up in the power
  you encourage me to claim, O Thea;

I shall teach them that goodness is stronger than evil,
  and love is stronger than hate.

In my integrity, support me, O Thea,
  and let your wisdom ever surround me.

Blessed be you, O Thea;
  blessed be all your Sacred Body.

Psalm 42

As the deer longs for running water
  so my flesh longs for you, O Thea.

I thirst for you, O Thea;
  when shall I perceive your presence?

My tears have been my food day and night.
  I pour out my heart when I think on these things:

How I went with the multitude
  and led them into the heart of you,
    with the voice of joy and thanksgiving.

Why are you so full of heaviness, O my flesh?
  and why are you so unsettled?

You offer your loving-kindness in the daytime, O Thea;
  in the night season your sweet song is with me.

Let your arms wrap close around me
  that I may remember that I am yours,
    flesh of your flesh.

Psalm 43

Rise up with me, O Thea;
  help me face those who act with unkindness.

Send out your light and your warmth through me,
  that their hearts may be touched.

Meet me eye to eye, nose to nose, face to face, O Thea,
  for you are my joy and gladness.

I trust in you, O Thea;
  and I rejoice that that trust is mutual.

Ninth Day: Morning Prayer

Psalm 44

Awake, O Thea!
  Why do you sleep? Arise!

Why have you forgotten my affliction and oppression?
  Even now I sink into the grave.

Help me, O Thea!
  save my life, for you are my last hope.

Psalm 45

My heart stirs with a vibrant song;
let me recite what I have fashioned;
   my tongue shall be the pen of a skilled writer.

You, O woman, are among the wise ones;
   grace flows from your lips.

Strap your sword upon your thigh, O mighty warrior,
   in your pride and in your skill.

Ride out in the cause of justice
   and for the sake of peace.

Your leadership shall endure,
   for you love goodness and reject unkindness.

Thea anoints you
   with the oil of gladness.

All your garments are fragrant
with myrrh, aloes, and cassia,
   and the music of strings makes you glad.

I will make your name to be remembered
   from one generation to another.

Psalm 46

We are Thea's Sacred Body,
   every creature's refuge and strength.

Therefore we will not fear, though the earth shakes,
   and though the mountains topple
   into the depths of the sea;

Though its waters rage and foam,
   and though great rocks tremble in the tumult.

Come and look upon Thea's works,
  what awesome things she has done
  through creation, her creatures.

She makes war to cease;
  she breaks the bow and shatters the spear.

"Be still, then;
  know that I am Thea
  and you are my Sacred Body."

Ninth Day: Evening Prayer

Psalm 47

Clap your hands!
  shout to Thea with a cry of joy.

Sing praises to Thea, sing praises;
  sing praises to her, sing praises!

For Thea authors all the universe;
  sing praises with all your skill.

All of creation is Thea's Sacred Body:
  holy, broken, and beautiful.

Psalm 48

All-embracing is Thea;
  creation is her Sacred Body.

Her creative joy reaches
to the universe's end and beyond;
  her limbs spill over with loving-kindness.

Thea journeys beside us always;
  she dances with us to the end of our days.

Psalm 49

Hear, all you who dwell in creation,
   old and young, rich and poor together.

My mouth shall speak of wisdom,
   and my heart shall meditate on understanding.

I will incline my ear to a proverb
   and set forth my riddle to music.

We see that the wealthy die as well as the unwealthy;
   they perish and leave their wealth
   to those who come after them.

Even though honored, they cannot live forever;
   they perish like all other creatures.

Though they thought highly of themselves while they lived,
   and were praised for their success,

They shall join the company of their forebears,
   and be changed forever in the depths of the earth.

For what treasure can we gather
   that even death will honor?

Tenth Day: Morning Prayer

Psalm 50

Thea speaks;
   her voice thunders through all the universe.

Thea comes and does not keep silence;
   all around her is an awesome storm.

She sees our wrongful deeds and says:
   "Why do you recite my wisdom,
   and take my covenant upon your lips;

Since you refuse the discipline to love,
    and toss my words behind your back?

You loosen your lips for evil,
    and harness your tongues to a lie.

Let your hearts be opened,
    so that you may journey the path of wisdom
    once more."

Psalm 51

Have mercy on me, O Thea,
according to your loving-kindness;
    in your compassion free me
    from the lure of wrongful deeds.

Wash the envy from my thoughts
    and guard me from all malice.

For I have come to recognize my wrongdoing,
    and my transgressions are before me.

Against you, against your Sacred Body,
    I have done what is harmful.

And so you are justified when you speak against me
    and upright in your judgment.

But behold, you look for truth deep within me,
    and will make me understand wisdom in stillness.

Make me hear of joy and gladness,
    that the Body that is broken may rejoice.

Create in me a clean heart, O Thea;
    renew me, for I am weary and worn.

Give me the joy of your help again
    and sustain me with your life-giving breath.

Then I shall teach others your ways,
and all who have strayed from the path of wisdom
shall return.

Deliver me from all that takes life, O Thea,
and I shall sing of you, my author and my love.

Psalm 52

Speak, you tyrant! Why do you boast of wickedness
against the oppressed all day long?

You plot ruin;
your tongue is like a sharpened blade,
O worker of deception.

You love evil more than good
and lying more than speaking the truth,

You love all words that hurt,
O you deceitful tongue.

Be still, that your eyes may be opened
to what you have done.
Turn from your evil deeds,
that your heart may be opened once more.

As for me, I have become a green olive tree
that flourishes at Thea's watering;
I will give thanks and proclaim
the potency of Thea's healing.

Tenth Day: Evening Prayer

Psalm 53

Thea looks upon creation, her Sacred Body,
to see if there is any who is wise.

"Do they not know, these creatures of mine,
  how they hurt and destroy
  those whom they are called to love?

But I shall wait,
and I shall enfold them in my embrace,
  until their hearts break free of their stony walls
  and throb again with living love."

Psalm 54

Hear me, O Thea;
  give ear to the words I speak.

For arrogant ones rise up against me,
  and those who are ruthless seek my ruin.

But you rescue me in the day of my trouble,
  and you save my life from danger.

When trouble visits me once more,
  I will breathe deeply and offer you thanks, O Thea,
  for you are with me.

You, O Thea, help me;
  you uphold my life.

Psalm 55

Listen to me, O Thea, and answer me;
  I have no peace, because of my cares.

 Oh, that I had wings like a dove!
  I would fly away and be at rest.

I would flee to a far-off place
  and make my lodging in the wilderness.

I would hasten to escape
  from the storm that swirls all around me.

Had it been an adversary who taunted me,
then I could have borne it;
  or had it been an enemy who vaunted herself against me,
  then I could have hidden from her.

But it was someone after my own heart,
  my companion, my own familiar friend.

We took sweet counsel together,
  and journeyed together on your way of wisdom.

Then my companion stretched forth her hand
against her dear one;
  she broke her covenant.

Her speech is softer than butter,
  but war is in her heart.

Her words are smoother than oil,
  but they are drawn swords.

But I will call upon you,
  and I trust that you will deliver me from this tempest.

O Thea, I cast upon you the burden I cannot bear,
  and I trust that you will lift me up once more.

Eleventh Day: Morning Prayer

Psalm 56

Strengthen me, O Thea,
  help me withstand the assaults that would shatter me.

All through the day my oppressors cause me harm.
They band together; they lie in wait;
  they spy upon my footsteps, seeking my ruin.

Nevertheless, I will honor the vow
  I made to your Sacred Body, O Thea:

I will journey beside you with a heart of empathy,
    offering a healing embrace to those whose suffer
    and to those who cause suffering.

Psalm 57

Enfold me, O Thea;
    I will take refuge in the shadow of your wings
    until this time of trouble has gone by.

For I lie in the midst of lions;
    their teeth are spears and arrows,
    their tongue a sharp sword.

You reach out your arms;
    you free me from my bonds with your limitless love.

And I shout, "Wake now, my flesh!
awake, strings and drums!
    I myself will waken the dawn!"

I will speak of you throughout creation, O Thea;
    I will sing my own song to you
    among my fellow creatures.

For your liberating power
has proven greater than the oceans,
    and your love reaches to the stars.

Psalm 58

Do you indeed decree righteousness, you rulers?
    do you judge the peoples with equity?

No; you devise evil in your hearts,
and your hands deal out violence
    against your fellow creatures,
    against the Sacred Body to which you belong.

Rulers who act wickedly are venomous as a serpent;
liars are like the deaf adder which stops its ears,
　　which does not heed the voice of the charmer,
　　no matter how skillful her charming.

May your judgments be like water that runs off;
　　may your power wither like trodden grass.

Before your influence bears fruit,
　　may it be cut down like a brier;
　　like thorns and thistles let it be swept away.

Eleventh Day: Evening Prayer

Psalm 59

Rouse yourself and come to my side, O Thea;
　　uphold me, for terror seizes me.

My eyes are fixed on you, O Thea!
　　Be my refuge in the midst of my trouble.

Help me find my voice,
that I may sing myself into strength, O Thea,
　　and celebrate your love at the break of day.

Psalm 60

O Thea, the earth shakes beneath our feet;
　　the ground beneath us splits in two.

Even the cedars and mountains are toppling;
　　who among us has any hope?

Give us courage, O Thea!
that we may remain steady and strong
　　in the midst of chaos,
　　and awaken tomorrow to see a new dawn.

Psalm 61

Hear me, O Thea;
  listen to my prayer.

For countless days I have lifted up my voice
  with heaviness in my heart.

But with each emerging day
I sing a new verse of your wisdom,
    learning each harmony in the song of your creation.

I will take refuge under the cover of your wings,
and sing the love song of your Sacred Body
    until I return to the depths
    and am transformed once more.

Twelfth Day: Morning Prayer

Psalm 62

For Thea alone do I wait in silence;
  truly my hope is in her.

She alone is my rock,
  my stronghold, so that I shall not be greatly shaken.

In Thea is my safety and my dignity;
  Thea is my strong rock and my refuge.

Steadfast love is hers,
  for she regards each creature
  according to her inestimable worth.

Psalm 63

O Thea, you are my lover; eagerly I seek you;
  my body thirsts for you, my flesh faints for you
  as in a dry, weary land without water.

Therefore I gaze upon your Sacred Body,
   that I might behold your power,
   your creative handiwork.

My flesh clings to yours;
   your hands hold mine fast.

Our love is better than life itself;
   we bless one another with joy.

When I think of you in our bed,
and meditate on you in the night,
   my flesh is content,
   and my mouth whispers of you with joyful lips.

You are my true love,
   and wrapped in your Sacred Body I rejoice.

Psalm 64

Hear my voice, O Thea;
   join me in dismantling the power of those who do harm.

Before me are those who nurture malice
   and aim their bitter words like arrows,

That they may shoot down their sister creatures in ambush;
   they shoot without warning and are not afraid.

They hold fast to their course;
   they plan how they may hide their snares.

May those blind with hatred trip over their weapons,
and may their eyes be opened
   that they may begin the journey
   that breaks their hearts open for love's planting.

Psalm 65

Happy are they, O Thea,
  who touch your Sacred Body!

You reveal your awesome wonders,
  the earth and the stars that paint the universe.

The mountains stand fast by your power;
  they are girded about with your might.

You still the roaring of the seas,
  and quiet the clamoring of the peoples.

Those who dwell near and far will tremble
as they taste your presence;
  the dawn and the dusk will sing for joy.

You water the earth,
you make it very plenteous;
  your river is full of living water.

You prepare the grain,
  providing for those who dwell on earth.

You drench the furrows and smooth out the ridges;
  with heavy rain you soften the ground
  and help its increase.

May the fields of the wilderness be rich for grazing,
  and the hills be clothed with joy.

May the meadows cover themselves with flocks,
  and the valleys cloak themselves with grain;

Let all of them shout for joy and sing
  as they partake of your presence, O Thea!

Psalm 66

Be joyful in Thea;
  sing a song of thanksgiving in her midst!

For when we were enslaved,
she turned the sea into dry land,
  so that we could journey safely
  through the waters to our liberation.

We moved through fire and water,
  emerging in a place of refreshment.

Blessed be Thea
who embraces and empowers
  those who are oppressed,
  every one.

Bless Thea with all your newfound strength;
  lift up your mighty voice and sing!

Psalm 67

O Thea, bless us, your creatures;
  reveal yourself through us and be present to us!

Let your wisdom be known throughout the universe,
  your healing love among us all.

May your Sacred Body be glad and sing for joy;
  and may all creation be revered!

Thirteenth Day: Morning Prayer

Psalm 68

We are glad and rejoice before you, O Thea;
  we are merry and playful!

We sing to you, rejoicing in you,
   exalting you as you glide through the vast oceans
   and ascend the jagged rocks!

Mother and defender of the vulnerable,
   you dwell within and among us!

You give the solitary one a home
   and usher prisoners to freedom.

You send a gracious rain upon the earth;
   you refresh the weary land.

Your creatures find their home in you, O Thea;
   in your goodness
   you embrace and empower the marginalized.

You have turned captivity captive;
   you lead us on the path of liberation.

Blessed be you, O Thea, day by day,
   for you bear our burdens and uplift us.

We move in a great procession, O Thea,
   singing songs of ecstatic joy.

The singers go before, musicians follow after,
   in the midst of young women playing the hand-drums.

We bless you, O Thea, in the gathering;
   we bless you, O Thea, for you are of the fountain of life.

You soar through the heavens,
the skies with their ancient lights;
   you send forth your mighty voice upon the waters.

We behold your power, O Thea;
   your majesty is woven through creation.

You are a well of wonders, O Thea,
   strengthening and empowering your Sacred Body!
   Blessed be you, O Thea!

Thirteenth Day: Evening Prayer

Psalm 69

Reach out and clasp my hands, O Thea,
    for the waters have risen up to my neck.

I am sinking into the miry depths,
    and there is no firm ground for my feet.

I have come into deep waters,
    and the torrent washes over me.

Those who see me murmur against me,
    and the drunkards make songs about me.

The reproach of others has broken my heart,
and it will not heal;
    I seek help, but there is none,
    I look for a comforter, but I can find no one.

But now I hear you whisper within me
that for the seed of change to bear fruit,
    I must seek fertile soil deep within myself;
    so this is my prayer, O Thea:

"In your wisdom, O Thea,
    let my broken heart remain open.

Save me from the mire; do not let me sink;
    rescue me out of the deep waters.

Let not the torrent of waters wash over me,
    nor let the deep swallow me up.

Reveal your path for me once more, O Thea,
for your love is kind;
    in your great compassion,
    guide and strengthen me."

Renewed with hope,
I will lift up my voice and sing, O Thea;
    I will bear new fruit with shouts of joy.

Psalm 70

O Thea, I beg you to make your love tangible;
    O Thea, journey by my side.

I am in greater need in this moment
than I have ever been;
    come to me speedily, O Thea.

You are my helper and my deliverer;
    O Thea, do not delay.

Fourteenth Day: Morning Prayer

Psalm 71

In you, O Thea, I take refuge;
    you are my muse and my safe haven.

I have been nurtured by you in secret
ever since I was born;
    from my mother's womb you have been my strength.

O Thea, you have taught me since I was young,
    and to this day I tell the stories of your wonders.

Time and again you have restored the fire within me
    bringing me up from the deep places
    where no one could see my light.

You deliver me from the hand that would ensnare me,
    from the clutches of my oppressor.

Therefore I will praise you, O Thea;
    I will sing to you with all the power of my voice,
    you who call me beloved.

My lips will sing when I play to you,
    and my body will tremble with joy
    as we join together in the dance.

Psalm 72

Teach your justice to the one who leads, O Thea,
  and your righteousness
  to those who follow in her stead.

She shall defend the needy among us;
  she shall rescue the poor and conquer the oppressor.

She shall come down like rain upon the mown field,
  like showers that water the earth.

In her time of leadership your creatures shall flourish;
  there shall be abundance of peace
  during every phase of the moon.

For she shall deliver those who cry out in distress,
  and the oppressed ones who have no helper.

She shall free their lives from violence,
  and dear shall they be in her sight.

May the name of the one who leads us
forever be a blessing
  and be established as long as the sun rises and falls;
  may the memory of her bless us forever.

Fourteenth Day: Evening Prayer

Psalm 73

Truly, Thea wishes peace of heart for her creatures,
  for all whom she has made.

But as for me, my feet had slipped;
  I had tripped and fallen;

I fell into envy of those who are unjust,
  and longed for the prosperity of those
  who profit from wrongdoing:

For they suffer no obvious pain,
 and their bodies are sleek and sound;

In the misfortunes of others they have no share;
 they are not afflicted as others are;

But they wear their pride like a necklace
 and wrap their disregard for others
 about them like a cloak.

They scoff and speak with disdain;
 in order to maintain their position,
 they plan oppression.

They set their mouths against other creatures,
 and their smooth speech runs through the world.

Despite this, others turn to them,
 in awe of their power, they find in them no fault.

As for me, I have broken my heart in vain;
 the reward for my open heart
 has been affliction all day long
 and punishment every morning.

When I try to understand these things,
 it is too hard for me.

My mind is embittered,
 and I am sorely wounded in my heart.

Yet you are always with me;
 you hold me close.

Whom do I have in creation but you?
 Whom do I desire but you, O Thea?

Envelop me in your wisdom, O Thea,
 and I shall find peace in you.

Psalm 74

O Thea, where are you in the midst of this chaos?
Turn your steps toward the endless ruins;
  our enemy has laid waste to everything.

There are no signs for us to see;
there is no prophetess left;
  there is not one among us
  who knows how long this will last.

How long, O Thea, will our adversary scoff?
  how long will our enemy oppress us?

Yet you are the maker of all, friend and enemy alike.
Yours is the day, yours also the night;
  you created the moon and the sun;
  you made both summer and winter.

Invest us with your healing, loving power, O Thea,
  that reconciliation may be made
  between us and our enemies;

Help us mend our broken lands and hearts,
  and we, no longer enemies,
  will sing songs of thanksgiving together.

Fifteenth Day: Morning Prayer

Psalm 75

We present ourselves to you, O Thea,
  calling upon you and trusting in your wisdom.

"The time has come," you say;
  "I will judge now with equity.

Judgment is neither from the east nor from the west,
  nor yet from the wilderness of the mountains.

It is I who judge;
  I weigh my creatures in the balance."

And when you have weighed each creature in your balance,
you will break open the hearts of those who act in evil ways,
   and nurture the hearts that are already open,
   so that all hearts may rejoice in freedom.

Psalm 76

Through your creatures you are known, O Thea,
   for your Sacred Body is creation.

As you speak,
   the earth stills itself in awe;

For as you sound your voice you spread out in love,
   reaching and liberating all who suffer in the margins.

Today I make my vow to you, O Thea;
today I use the poignant power of my voice:
   I swear that as long as I breathe,
   I will journey on your path of radical love.

Psalm 77

I cry aloud to you, O Thea;
   I cry aloud, that you might hear me.

My eyelids will not stay closed;
   I am deeply troubled and cannot sleep.

My heart whispers despair in the night;
   I weep and search my mind.

Has your loving-kindness come to an end, O Thea?
   have you broken your promise?

But then I remember your works,
   and call to mind your wonders.

I meditate on your acts
   and ponder your powerful deeds.

The waters tremble, O Thea;
  their very depths shake.

The clouds pour out water;
the skies thunder;
  arrows of light flash here and there;

The sound of thunder cracks in the whirlwind;
lightning lights up the world;
  the earth trembles and shakes.

Flowers blossom in the desert
  and strangers offer shelter from the cold.

When all hope seems lost,
  your Sacred Body forges a path.

I remember your deeds, O Thea,
and hope glimmers ahead;
  thus I shall not despair,
  but continue to journey at your side.

Fifteenth Day: Evening Prayer

Psalm 78

Hear my teaching, my sisters,
  incline your ears to my words.

I will open my mouth in a parable;
  I will declare the mysteries of old.

That which we have heard and known,
and what our foremothers have told us,
  we will not hide from our children.

We will recount to generations to come
  the loving power of Thea.

She established wisdom,
  which she gave us to teach our children;

That the generations to come might learn it,
  and they in their turn might tell it to their children;

So that they might discover their divine identity
  as her Sacred Body.

She worked marvels in the sight of our foremothers,
  in the land where they were once enslaved.

She split open the sea and let them pass through;
  she made the waters stand up like walls.

She led them with a cloud by day,
  and all the night through with a glow of fire.

She split the hard rocks in the wilderness
  and quenched their thirst.

She brought streams out of the cliff,
  and the waters gushed out like rivers.

And she said to them, "This!
  This is what I do for you,
  what I want you to do for all creatures!"

But they strayed from the path she had given them,
  rebelling in the desert against her.

They tested her in their hearts,
  demanding food for their craving.

They railed against her and said,
  "Can you set a table in the wilderness?

True, when the rock was struck, the waters gushed forth;
  but what of bread to sustain us?"

When Thea heard this,
  a fire ignited in her heart,

For they had no faith in Thea;
  how could they possibly have faith in themselves?

So she showed them again her power,
  that they might glimpse what lay within themselves.

She sent fresh rains for their spring planting
and warm sunlight for summer growing
  so there would be ripe grain for an autumn reaping:
  She provided for them all they needed.

She let it grow in the midst of them
  and round about their dwellings.

So they were well filled,
  for she gave them what they needed.

But they did not believe in their own promise,
  that her power to work miracles was also their power.

They remained steadfast in their stubbornness
  and had no understanding of her wonderful works.

Then Thea arose as though from sleep,
  like a warrior refreshed with wine.

She set her eyes on her creatures,
  whom she had always loved;

And she whispered in their hearts once more,
that they might recognize
  their true calling, their deepest yearning,
  and become her miracle-working hands, feet, and heart.

Sixteenth Day: Morning Prayer

Psalm 79

O Thea, there are some among us
who have overpowered us;
  they have made our homes a pile of rubble.

These ones, who are as beloved by you
as those of us they harm,
  they have given our lives as food for the birds of the air,
  and our flesh to the animals of the field.

They have shed our blood like water on every side,
  and there has been no one left to bury the dead.

We are exhausted and despairing, O Thea;
let your compassion be swift to meet us!
  Let your great love prevail over your Sacred Body;
  then we will have hope of living in peace once more.

Psalm 80

Hear us, O gardener of creation;
  heed the call of our voices!

You brought forth a great vine.
You prepared the ground for it;
  it took root and filled the land.

The mountains were covered by its shadow
  and the towering cedar trees by its boughs.

You stretched out its tendrils to the sea
  and its branches to the river.

So why have you watched
and done nothing as its support crumbled,
  allowing it to slump
  and be crushed under its own weight?

Turn now, O Thea, and look;
  behold and tend the vine you planted.

Bestow your self-nurturing power upon us,
  for we are your Sacred Body.

Restore us, O Thea,
  that your vine may bear good fruit for food and wine;
  and then all will eat and drink and be satisfied.

Psalm 81

Thea said,
"You called on me when you were hungry,
  and I answered you from the secret place of thunder.

I said, 'Open your mouth wide,
  that I may satisfy your hunger.'

But you did not hear my voice;
  you would not listen to me.

You chose instead to steal and hoard,
  robbing others and leaving them to starve.

If only you would open your ears and hear!
  If only you would open your eyes and see!
  If only you would open your hearts and love as I do!

Then you would understand
that there is food enough for all,
  and that while any is lacking, all lack.

You would learn to give, not to hoard;
  and you would learn that in giving,
  you receive all that you need."

Sixteenth Day: Evening Prayer

Psalm 82

Thea speaks in the great council of creation;
  she gives judgment in the midst of the powerful:

"How long will you judge unjustly,
  and show favor to those who act wickedly?

Save the weak and vulnerable;
  defend the humble and needy;

Rescue the poor;
    deliver them from the power of the oppressor.

You are powerful,
    and all of you are my creatures,
    burning brightly with the light I have planted in you;

Nevertheless you shall die,
    and fall like any ruler.

Arise, all you who are wise;
listen to me, and I will teach you
    to journey along my path,
    leading creation forward in love."

Psalm 83

O Thea, do not be silent;
    for the sake of your Sacred Body, do not keep quiet;

For there are those who conspire together;
    they are making an alliance against your Sacred Body,
    against their own home, creation.

O Thea, make their plans like whirling dust,
    and like chaff before the wind;

Like fire that burns down a forest,
    like the flame that sets mountains ablaze.

Shock them all with a storm,
    and drive their vision away with a tempest;

That your Sacred Body may live on,
    bearing your love from age to age.

Psalm 84

How dear to me is your dwelling-place, O Thea!
    I long for your lands and seas and starfire;
    I rejoice in you.

The sparrow has found herself a house
and the swallow a nest where she may lay her young
    by the sides of the altar
    where I offer my prayers, O Thea.

Happy are the people whose strength is in you!
    whose hearts are set on the pilgrims' way.

Those who go through the desolate valley
will find it a place of springs,
    for the early rains have covered it
    with fresh pools of water.

They will climb from height to height,
    and you will reveal yourself in them.

Psalm 85

Show us your wisdom, O Thea,
    and grant us your understanding.

Truly, both wisdom and understanding
are near to those who seek you,
    for your wisdom manifests throughout creation,
    your Sacred Body.

Behold, mercy and truth shall meet!
    Justice and peace shall kiss!

Likewise, truth shall spring up from the earth,
    and righteousness shall look down from the skies.

Goodness shall lead us,
    and peace shall be our pathway.

As we journey,
wisdom will grow like wildfire in our hearts,
    and we will learn to understand one another as you do.

Psalm 86

O Thea, tend the fire of my life;
  guard my flame, for I trust in you.

Give ear, O Thea, to my prayer,
  and attend to the sound of my voice.

In times of trouble I call upon you,
  and I trust that you will answer.

Show me your loving-kindness, O Thea,
  just as you have helped me and comforted me before.

Great is your love toward me;
  even now, you deliver me from the turbulent waters
  that would extinguish my light.

Teach me your way, O Thea,
and I will journey in your truth;
  knit my heart to yours,
  that I may learn the pattern of your ways.

Psalm 87

All that is within and beyond the universe
dwells in Thea;
  she loves you with the greatest love, O creation!

Glorious things are spoken of you, O Sacred Body;
  everyone and everything was born in you.

The singers and the dancers
will sing and shout to you, O creation:
  "All my fresh springs are in you."

Psalm 88

O Thea, with each day and night
   I cry to you.

Let my voice enter your mind;
   incline your ear to my words.

For I am full of trouble;
   my life is at the brink.

Your absence weighs upon me heavily,
   and great waves of fear overwhelm me.

My friends are far from me;
   I am imprisoned and cannot get free.

I call upon you daily;
   I stretch out my hands to you.

O Thea, where may I find you?
   why do you hide your face from me?

Ever since my youth,
   I have borne your absence
   with a troubled, desperate mind.

Your absence has swept over me;
   your absence destroys me;

It surrounds me all day long like a flood,
   encompassing me on every side.

My friend and my neighbor are far from me,
   and darkness is my only companion.

O Thea, draw near to me at last;
   O Thea, scatter my darkness.

Psalm 89

I will sing of your love forever, O Thea;
    from this day forth my mouth will sing of you.

For I am convinced that your love is for us all,
every last one of us;
    you have enveloped all creation in it.

Creation bears witness to your wonders, O Thea,
    and to your love in our gatherings.

Righteousness and justice
are the bones of your Sacred Body;
    love and truth are the contours of your face.

Happy are the people who know the festal shout!
    they journey, O Thea,
    in the loving light of your presence.

Truly, you lead us;
    you, the Holy One of creation,
    guide us in our paths.

In every age, in every place,
you say to your beloved creatures:
    "I place my hands on the head of an artist
    and exalt one chosen from among you.

With my holy oil I anoint her;
    she will guide you in my ways.

My hand holds her fast
    and my arm makes her strong.

She is not easily deceived,
    and sloth will not bring her down.

My imagination and creativity are with her,
    and her life's story shall be told
    as one of great fruitfulness.

She says to me, 'You are my author
  and the sure ground beneath me.'

She will nurture, challenge, and lead you,
  and through her my great love will be revealed."

Blessed be you, O Thea,
  and blessed be your chosen one among us!

Eighteenth Day: Morning Prayer

Psalm 90

O Thea, you have been our refuge
  from one generation to another.

We long for bliss as we know it to go on forever,
but you turn us back to the dust and say,
  "Go back, O child of earth."

For a thousand years in your sight
are like yesterday when it is past,
  and like a watch in the night.

You sweep us away like a dream;
  we fade away suddenly like the grass.

In the morning it is green and flourishes;
  in the evening it is dried up and withered.

The span of a human life is seventy years,
perhaps in strength even eighty,
  but your Sacred Body has lived
  and changed through every age.

So teach us to number our days
  that we may apply our hearts to wisdom.

Satisfy us by your loving-kindness in the morning;
  then we may rejoice and be glad
  all the days of our life.

May your gracious vision be revealed to us;
  may the work of our hands be marked by your love.

Psalm 91

You who dwell in Thea's haven
  abide in the cove of the mighty one.

And you say to Thea,
"You are my refuge and my strength,
  my muse in whom I trust."

Thea will guard the flame of your calling
from those who would extinguish it,
  and you will find safe refuge in her hollow;
  her faithful presence will be your cloak.

You shall not fear any terror by night,
  nor the arrow that flies by day;

The plague that stalks in the darkness,
  nor the sickness that lays waste at noon.

For she will place you in the company of wise ones,
  to help you in all your ways.

They will guide you on difficult paths,
  lest you slip and fall into a trap.

Thea says of you, "She is bound to me in love;
  I will journey with her, because I love her.

I will accompany her in her doubt
  and help her return to confidence
  with newfound wisdom.

With the fullness of life I will satisfy her,
  and reveal to her my wild, evergreen love."

Psalm 92

It is a good thing to lift up my voice to you, O Thea,
   to tell of your loving-kindness in the morning
   and of your enveloping presence in the night;

On the woodwind, on the drums,
   and to the melody of the strings.

For you have made me glad, O Thea;
   and I shout for joy at the works of your hands.

You shall seek out the young as well as the broken-hearted
and to them you shall offer your seeds for new planting;
   through them, your love shall flourish like a palm tree,
   and shall spread abroad like a cedar.

The seeds of your love shall bear fruit in old age,
   fruit that is sweet and succulent;

And those who are offered this fruit
   will taste it and hunger for more.

To those who hunger,
you shall offer your seeds for planting,
   and the cycle will start anew.

In this way your love will flourish
   until all of creation is fed.

Eighteenth Day: Evening Prayer

Psalm 93

O Thea, you have put on splendid apparel
   and clothed yourself with strength.

The waters have lifted up,
the waters have lifted up their voice;
   the waters have lifted up
   their pounding waves to you, O Thea.

Mightier than the sound of many waters,
mightier than the breakers of the seas,
   mightier are you who dwell within and among us.

You are dressed in rich folds of wisdom, O Thea,
   and holiness adorns your Sacred Body.

Psalm 94

How long, O Thea,
   how long shall those who act wickedly triumph?

O Thea, can a corrupt community
have any part with you,
   a community that frames evil into wisdom?

Can they pray to you,
those who conspire against the life of the just
   and condemn the innocent to death?

Can they call your name,
those who murder the stranger
   and abandon the vulnerable to die?

Surely their wickedness will turn back upon them
   until their own wrongdoing eats them up.

Only then will their prayer to you be sincere;
   despite their previous hard-heartedness,
   you will not conceal yourself from them;

For you will not abandon any of your creatures,
innocent or not;
   nor will you forsake the universe.

As often as I said, "I am slipping,"
   your love, O Thea, upheld me.

O Thea, teach those who journey in unjust ways
to turn to your path of wisdom;
   call wrongdoers away from the path of hatred.

For when we open our ears and hear your voice,
   we will turn toward you in a slow, aching ecstasy,
   longing for nothing else but to journey with you once more.

We will behold one another with new eyes;
   we will see that we are all members of your Sacred Body,
   and we will revere one another, we will revere you, anew.

Nineteenth Day: Morning Prayer

Psalm 95

Come, let us sing to Thea;
   let us shout for joy to our rock.

Let us journey in her presence with thanksgiving
   and raise a loud shout to her with psalms.

For in her hands are the caverns of the earth,
   and the heights of the hills are hers also.

The sea is her creation,
   and her hands ever yet mold the dry land.

Come! as sweet incense rises all around us,
   let us bend low, revering Thea our author.

Thea is our muse,
   and we are her Sacred Body.

Psalm 96

Sing to Thea a new song;
   sing to her with a strong voice!

Sing to Thea and bless her;
   bless her Sacred Body, creation.

Oh, the majesty and the magnificence of her!
   Oh, the might and the splendor of her!

Wonder at Thea's beauty;
   let the whole universe tremble.

Let the heavens rejoice and the earth be glad;
let the seas and all that is in them thunder;
   let the trees of the woods
   and all that dwell in them sound a joyful noise.

From the hidden places of the earth
to the hidden wonders of the universe,
   all shall shout for joy
   to Thea, our author and Sacred Body.

Psalm 97

Thea is all that is, all that has been, and all that will be;
   clouds and shadow whirl round about her,
   righteousness and justice stream from her limbs.

Her lightning lights up the world;
   the earth trembles and quakes.

The mountains melt like wax at the sound of her voice,
   at the voice of Thea whose Sacred Body is the universe.

Creation beholds Thea and is glad,
   enveloped in her unrelenting love.

Rejoice in Thea, you creatures;
   give thanks for the One you are, O Sacred Body!

Nineteenth Day: Evening Prayer

Psalm 98

Sing a new song to Thea,
   for she has done marvelous things.

With her hands, the touch of her fingers,
   she liberates her Sacred Body.

Shout with joy to Thea, all you lands;
    lift up your voice, rejoice, and sing.

Sing to Thea with the strum of strings,
    with the strings and the voice of song.

With trumpets and the sound of the horn,
    shout with joy before her.

Let the seas make a clamorous noise,
    the lands and those who dwell there.

Let the rivers clap their hands
    and the hills ring out with joy in Thea!

Psalm 99

Proclaim the marvels of Thea;
    she is the Holy One, and we are her Sacred Body.

Miriam was among her priestesses;
    she called upon Thea, and Thea answered her.

Thea speaks to all her beloved ones;
    they keep to the path she gives them.

Thea hears and answers us indeed;
    she empowers us in her great love.

Proclaim the greatness of Thea;
    for she is the Holy One, and we are her Sacred Body.

Psalm 100

Be joyful in Thea, all you creatures;
    journey with her gladly,
    revering her with a song.

Know this: Thea herself is in and of us all;
    we are her Sacred Body and her true delight.

Embrace the passion she has planted in you;
 accept her deepest call for your life,
 and she will be your faithful muse.

Psalm 101

I will sing of mercy and justice;
 O Thea, I will sing of your love.

I will strive to follow a blameless course;
 I will journey with a sincere heart.

A hardened heart shall be far from me;
 I will not foster malice.

I will transform others as I journey on this path we share;
 and in your power I will heal those whom I touch.

Twentieth Day: Morning Prayer

Psalm 102

O Thea, incline your ear to me;
 when I call, make haste to answer me,

I weep all day long,
 and I am but skin and bones.

I have become like a vulture in the wilderness,
 like an owl among the ruins.

I lie awake through the night, unable to find rest;
 I am like a sparrow, lonely on a housetop.

For I have eaten ashes for bread
 and mingled my drink with tears.

My days pass like a shadow,
 and I wither like grass in the desert.

But you, O Thea, you will practice compassion;
   you are an oasis in the desert.

You perceive the many facets of your Sacred Body;
   you behold all you have made and become.

Let this be written for future generations,
   so that your tales and songs may deliver comfort.

You will answer the prayer of those who have no home;
   you will co-create a fitting dwelling with them.

You will soothe the cries of those giving new birth
   and serve as midwife to those bearing the pangs of death.

Your every-changing creation shall continue,
   and your Sacred Body shall thrive.

Psalm 103

Bless Thea, O my flesh,
   and all that is within me, bless her nearness.

She comforts me when death draws near
   and crowns me with love;

She blesses me with gratitude,
   and renews my energy like an eagle's.

As a mother cares for her children,
   so does Thea care for those she nurtures into being.

For she herself knows what we are made of;
   she remembers that we are dust.

Our days are like the grass;
   we flourish like a flower of the field;

When the wind goes over it, it is gone,
   making way for new grasses, new flowering.

Bless Thea, all you whom she has made;
  bless Thea, O my flesh.

Twentieth Day: Evening Prayer

Psalm 104

Bless Thea, O my flesh;
  O Thea, how marvelous you are!
  your Sacred Body is creation, both vast and diverse.

You make the winds your messengers
  and flames of fire your beacons.

You set the earth in motion,
  orbiting one of your many great lights.

Your springs descend to the valleys;
  they flow between the mountains.

All the animals of the field drink their fill from them,
  and from them we, too, quench our thirst.

In the nearby trees the birds of the air make their nests
  and sing among the branches.

Waters spring from the mountains from above;
  the earth bears all manner of fruit.

You make grass grow for flocks and herds
  and plants to feed us all;

You teach us all
  we need to live a holy life:

To fill a glass,
  that dry lips may be moistened,

To anoint with oil the body
  that has only begun to know its own holy power,

And to make bread for feasting,
  that unjust hunger might die.

Your trees are full of sap,
  the cedars which you planted,

In which the birds build their nests,
  and in whose tops the stork makes her dwelling.

The high hills are a refuge for the mountain goats,
  and the stony cliffs for the rock badgers.

By the moon we mark the seasons,
  and we mark the day by the sun's rising and setting.

You blanket your Sacred Body in darkness
so that day creatures may have the relief of night
  and night creatures may wake to make their playful way.

O Thea, how diverse are the works of your hands!
  in wisdom you have created all we know and more;
  the universe is full of your imagining.

Beyond is the great and wide sea
with living things too many to number,
  creatures both small and great.

All of us look to you
  for food in due season.

You teach us to plant that for which we hunger;
  thus we are filled with the harvest of our own planting.

You receive our last breath,
  and we die, returning to the dust.

You send forth your breath into the dust once more;
  and so you renew the face of the earth.

May your wonders inspire forever;
  may joy echo in all you have brought to birth.

I will sing to you as long as I live, O Thea;
   I will honor you with every breath.

Bless Thea, O my flesh.
   Hallelujah!

Twenty-first Day: Morning Prayer

Psalm 105

Call upon Thea and offer to do her holy work,
   that her wonders might be worked in every place.

Thea chose Miriam to lead us,
   for she was wise and imaginative,
   powerful and empowering.

Thea worked her miracles through Miriam,
   her wonders among us.

Miriam led our dance to freedom,
   lifting her voice to shatter the silence
   imposed by our oppressors.

Then Thea spread out a cloud as a covering for us,
   and a fire to give light in the enduring night.

We asked, and food appeared,
   and she satisfied us with a feast of her own making.

She split the impenetrable boulder, and water flowed,
   so that water coursed through in dry places.

Miriam, her faithful priestess,
   taught us Thea's many wonders:

Healing, listening, mending, weaving,
   reconciling, dancing, and feeding.

All these were our way-food
   on the journey to wisdom.

Thea looks ever among us for the wise and imaginative,
the powerful and empowering,
   through whom she can work her wonders
   and reveal her delight in creation.

Twenty-first Day: Evening Prayer

Psalm 106

We give thanks to you, O Thea,
   for your loving care does not cease.

When we were enslaved
   we forgot your marvelous works.

We did not remember the abundance of your love;
   we turned to despair,
   believing not even you could help us.

But you set us free,
   making your power known.

You rebuked the sea, and it dried up,
   you led us through the deep as through a desert.

You delivered us from the hand of those
who belittled and used us,
   empowered us to escape
   from those who would have held us captive.

But we soon forgot your help
   and did not take time
   to discern your wisdom for ourselves.

We forgot you, O Thea,
   you who had liberated us.

We grumbled in our beds
   and would not listen to your voice.

Then we were overtaken once more
   and hatred ruled over us.

Our fears oppressed us,
   and we were humiliated into inaction.

Time after time
you delivered us from our enslavement,
   but we forgot your love and sank into new traps.

Nevertheless, you saw our distress.
   when we voiced our lamentation.

You exercised your loving liberation,
even when we forgot it,
   and you opened wide the gates
      that had appeared as insurmountable walls.

Blessed be you, O Thea, author of creation,
   and may the blessing of your love ever be upon us!

Twenty-second Day: Morning Prayer

Psalm 107

Give thanks to Thea,
for her love is a holy flame
   that burns brightly within her creatures.

Some wander in the desert,
   finding no way to a city
      where their hearts might dwell.

They hunger and thirst;
   their flesh languishes.

Then they look within themselves for Thea's help,
   and their own divine fire melts their icy fear;

Thea thus sets them on a straight path
   to go to a city where they might dwell.

Some sit in darkness and deep gloom,
  bound fast in misery;

They are humbled with difficult work;
  they stumble and find none to help.

Then they look within themselves for Thea's help,
  and their own divine fire melts their icy fear;

Thea thus leads them
out of darkness and deep gloom
  and breaks their bonds asunder.

Some go down to the sea in ships
  and ply their trade in deep waters;

Then a stormy wind rises up,
  which tosses high the waves of the sea.

They mount up to the skies
and fall back to the depths;
  their hearts freeze because of their peril.

They reel and stagger like drunkards
  and are at their wits' end.

Then they look within themselves for Thea's help,
  and their own divine fire melts their icy fear;

Thea thus stills the storm to a whisper
  and she brings them to the harbor
  for which they are bound.

Thea's love changes deserts into pools of water
  and dry land into water-springs.

She settles the hungry there,
  and they find a city where they can dwell.

They sow fields, and plant vineyards,
  and bring in a fruitful harvest.

The wise will ponder these things,
   and consider well the holy fire of Thea
   that burns within.

Twenty-second Day: Evening Prayer

Psalm 108

My heart clings fast to you, O Thea;
   you sweeten the song of my lips.

Awake, O my flesh;
wake now, drum and harp;
   I myself will waken the dawn.

I will reveal you with all the skill of my art, O Thea;
   I will praise you with my fingers, my feet, my breath.

For your promise is greater than the mountains,
   and your love is deeper than the deepest valley.

Psalm 109

Do not fail to act, O Thea,
   while the mouth of the one who hates me
   opens against me.

She speaks to me with a lying tongue;
   she surrounds me with hateful words
   and fights against me without a cause.

Despite my love, she accuses me;
   but as for me,
   I pray that your love will envelop her.

She repays evil for good,
   and hatred for my love.

She does not remember to show mercy,
  but persecutes the poor and needy
  and seeks to destroy the brokenhearted.

She loves cursing,
but let it not come upon her;
  she takes no delight in blessing,
  but let it shower upon her.

She wears cursing like a garment,
  let it not soak into her body like water
  or into her bones like oil;

Let it not be to her like the cloak
which she wraps around herself,
  and like the belt that she wears continually.

O Thea, midwife of all creation,
  for your tender mercy's sake, deliver her.

For she is poor and needy,
  and her heart is wounded within her.

She has faded away
like a shadow when it lengthens;
  she is shaken off like a locust.

Her knees are weak,
  and her flesh is wasted and gaunt.

She has become a reproach to all around her;
  they see and shake their heads.

Help her, O Thea;
  heal her for your mercy's sake.

She may curse, but you will bless;
  give her cause to rejoice once more.

Then I will give great thanks to you with my mouth;
  in the midst of the multitude I will praise you;

Because you stand beside the one who is most needy,
  to deliver her from her own stony heart.

Twenty-third Day: Morning Prayer

Psalm 110

You, O Thea, said to me,
"Let us sit side by side."

You have invested creation, your Sacred Body,
with your power, saying,
  "In the beauty of holiness I have created you,
  like dew from the womb of the morning."

You have sworn to me and you will not recant:
  "You are a priestess forever.

Now go forth and reveal my love
  with touch, taste, sound,
  sight, smell, and story;

Love, illumine, and empower your kindred creatures
  with all the might and beauty of your gifts."

Psalm 111

I give thanks to Thea with my whole heart,
  shouting in the gathering of her creatures.

Great are her deeds!
  all who delight in them study them.

She gives food to those who hunger;
  she offers her cup to those who thirst.

The works of her hands are justice and love,
  her path is deep joy.

Beholding Thea is the beginning of wisdom;
　　behold her, and understanding shall be yours.

Psalm 112

Happy is the one who beholds Thea
　　and takes delight in her wisdom!

Light shines in the darkness
for the one who seeks it;
　　she who cultivates wisdom
　　is merciful and full of compassion.

She will never be shaken;
　　no, she will not topple.

Her heart opens;
　　she puts her trust in Thea.

She gives freely to those in need,
　　and she honors others with her integrity.

The one who does evil deeds will see it
and a seed shall be planted;
　　her wicked desires will wither and perish,
　　and wisdom will grow hardy in their stead.

Psalm 113

Give praise, you priestesses of Thea;
　　praise Thea with the fruit of your labor.

Bless Thea;
　　let all her Sacred Body bless.

From the rising of the sun to its setting
　　honor Thea with your prophetic, imaginative works.

Psalm 114

When we were freed from our bondage,
    newly freed from the bonds that limited us,

The sea felt its freedom and fled;
    The rivers turned and went back.

The mountains skipped like rams
    and the little hills like young sheep.

The hard rock turned to pools of water
    and flint-stone into flowing springs.

Tremble, O creatures, at the liberation of Thea,
    at the freedom of the one
    whose Sacred Body we are.

Psalm 115

You who seek Thea, trust in Thea;
    she beholds you in her great love.

She blesses those who behold her,
    who witness and revere her holy presence
    in every creature.

Let us bless every creature we behold,
    for it is we, Thea's creatures,
    who are the Sacred Body that blesses.

Twenty-fourth Day: Morning Prayer

Psalm 116

Hear my voice, O Thea;
    incline your ear to me,

For the ropes of death entangle me,
    and the grip of the grave takes hold of me.

But I trust that you will rescue
my life from destruction,
    my eyes from tears,
    and my body from stumbling.

For your kindness is mighty;
    your compassion envelops weakness
    and conceives new strength.

Even now, you give me a new opportunity
to journey in your presence
    in the land of the living.

O Thea, I am yours;
    I am the daughter of your daughters.

I will fulfill my vow to journey on your path
    in the presence of my kindred creatures.

I will lift up the cup of your promise
    and seek you in al creation, O Thea.

Psalm 117

Honor Thea with all your creativity;
    shout and dance for joy!

Her love overflows from us;
    for we are her Sacred Body.
    Hallelujah!

Psalm 118

Journey with Thea, for she is playful and wise;
    her creative love endures through every age.

When Thea is at my side, I do not fear;
    for what can anyone do to me?

Those who are unkind may encompass me;
  but with the skill of Thea I will heal them.

They swarm about me like bees;
  they blaze like a fire of thorny vines;
  but in the name of Thea I will heal them.

Thea is my strength and my song;
  she is my courage and my help.

I shall not waste away, but bear lasting fruit,
  embracing Thea's imagination
  with my whole life.

"Hosanna, hosanna!
  Behold! the one who will lead us emerges!

Blessed are you who come in the name of Thea;
  we bless you from throughout creation.

Thea shines upon you and from you;
we form a procession
  with colorful branches held high,
  that you may enter our circle with honor."

Journey with Thea, for she is playful and wise;
  her creative love endures through every age.

Twenty-fourth Day: Evening Prayer

Psalm 119

A

Happy is she whose path is playful,
  who journeys in your imaginative ways, O Thea!

Happy is she who beholds you
  and dances with you with all her heart!

Who refuses what is dull,
    and instead imagines as you do.

You offer your wisdom, O Thea,
    that we should fully explore it.

I will honor your path with heart wide open;
    I will journey by your side.

O Thea, illumine my path
    with all the vibrant hues of your love.

B

How shall a young woman
clear the rocky path before her?
    By drawing on your joyful wisdom for strength.

I stoke your creative flame in my heart;
    may I never fail to tend this holy fire.

With my lips I will sing
    all the wisdom of your mouth.

I have taken greater delight in your imaginative ways
    than in all manner of riches.

I will meditate on your joyful wisdom
    and give attention to your ways.

My delight is in journeying with you;
    I will ever seek your inspiration.

C

Show me your playful love, O Thea,
    so that I may learn it and offer it to those I meet.

Open my eyes that I may see
    the wonders of your creativity.

I am a stranger here;
  reveal your path for me.

I am consumed at all times
  with longing for your wisdom.

Protect me from acting out of spite or despair;
  guide me on your creative path.

For your path is my delight,
  you are my muse and my counselor.

D

My flesh cleaves to you;
  guide me life according to your wisdom.

I lay bare my life, and you inspire me;
  lead me in the path of your wisdom.

Make me understand the way of your love,
  that I may make meditations of your marvels.

When I feel weak, unable to move forward,
  strengthen me according to your love.

Take from me the way of sloth and harm;
  let me find grace through play.

I honor the covenant we share;
  I set the good of your Sacred Body
  above solitary gain.

O Thea, invite me to join the dance.
Though I am uncertain,
  I will move joyfully for I am with you.

I will fly in your creativity,
  for you set my heart free.

E

Teach me, O Thea, the beauty of your imagination,
  and I shall cultivate it to the end of my days.

Show me how to plant your creativity,
  and I shall nurture it with all my heart.

Guide me in pursuing my heart's path,
  for faithfulness to your creative ways
  is my desire.

Incline my heart to the good of your Sacred Body
  and not to unjust gain.

Teach me to take hold of my gifts
  for the sake of wisdom and joy.

O Thea, I long to be fruitful as you are;
  give me life in your ways.

F

Let your loving-kindness be my food, O Thea,
  and your playful love wrap about me like a cloak.

I will journey freely,
  because I am faithful to your ways.

I will share your wisdom before rulers
  and will not be ashamed.

I delight in your path,
  which I have always loved.

In the morning and in the evening,
I will lift up my hands in prayer
  and meditate on your wisdom.

Twenty-fifth Day: Morning Prayer

G

Remember your promise to your beloved, O Thea;
  you give me hope.

I meditate on your wisdom
as I bear the fruit of creativity,
  and in your wisdom I take great comfort.

Your ways have been songs to me
  wherever I have lived as a stranger.

I remember you in the stillness, O Thea,
  and breathe in your wisdom.

H

You are my portion and my cup, O Thea;
  you nourish me from your breast.

I move forward, though I am uncertain,
  and I seek your path when I lose my way.

Though doubts entangle me,
  I remember your steadfast encouragement.

The universe, O Thea, is your Sacred Body;
  teach me to love all of you as you do.

I

O Thea, teach me discernment and courage,
  for I trust in your love.

You are good and you bring forth good;
  guide me in your ways.

The wisdom of your Sacred Body
is more precious to me
    than millions in silver and gold.

J

You grant me understanding of your imagination,
    that I may bear your wisdom into the world.

Let your loving creativity be my hope,
    and your playful wisdom my comfort.

Let my heart be shaped with your love,
    that I may be your living icon.

K

My flesh longs for you, O Thea;
    draw close to me in your love.

Your passion gives me breath;
    fill and surround me with your wisdom.

In your love, bring me to life,
    and I will hold you close forever.

Twenty-fifth Day: Evening Prayer

L

O Thea, your love for me is everlasting,
    for I am the work of your hands.

I love your Sacred Body;
    I am yours.

All else may come to an end,
    but your love will endure.

M

Oh, how I love your wisdom!
  you consume me.

Your path makes me wiser
  and is always before me.

I have more understanding
than my teachers,
  for your ways are my study.

I am wiser than my elders,
  because I journey along your path.

How sweet are your words when I taste them!
  they are sweeter than honey to my mouth.

Through your wisdom I gain understanding;
  therefore I rebel against every unjust way.

N

Your love is a lantern to my heart
  and a light upon my path.

I have vowed and am determined
  to keep to your ways.

Hear, O Thea, the whispers of my lips,
  and teach me your wisdom.

Your love is my inheritance forever;
  truly, you are the joy of my heart.

I apply my heart to fulfill your loving vision
  for all the rest of my days.

O

I once nurtured a divided heart,
   but now I devote myself
   wholly to your wisdom.

You are my refuge and courage;
   my hope is in your Sacred Body.

Empower me according to your covenant,
   and encourage me to trust in hope.

Hold me fast, and I shall be secure,
   and my delight shall ever be in you.

P

I am at the service of your loving vision;
   grant me understanding
   beyond what I now perceive.

Truly, I love your wisdom
   more than gold and glittering stones.

Yet it is time for you to act, O Thea,
   for others have not yet felt
   your healing touch.

Teach me to be your icon, O Thea,
   and then I shall illumine their hearts
   with your love.

Twenty-sixth Day: Morning Prayer

Q

Your wisdom is wonderful;
   therefore I listen to you with all my heart.

I open my mouth, craving you;
   I thirst for you, O Thea.

Steady me when I tremble;
   journey with me on my path.

Empower me to break free from all that harms,
   and grant me the wisdom to love as you do.

Let your love shine through my creative work,
   so that others may behold you and be glad.

R

I am small and of little account, O Thea
   yet I do not forget your command to love.

Your love is an unrelenting love,
   and your wisdom is more precious
   than priceless gems.

Even when trouble and distress come upon me,
   your wisdom is my delight.

Your kindness is everlasting;
   grant me understanding,
   that I may love as you do.

S

I call to you with my whole heart;
   answer me, O Thea,
   that I may keep your ways.

Early in the morning I cry out to you,
   for I put my trust in your wisdom.

My eyes are open in the night,
   that I may meditate upon your promise.

Hear me, O Thea, according to your loving-kindness;
 according to your wisdom, give me life.

T

Great is your compassion, O Thea;
 sustain me in your creativity.

O Thea, how I love you!
 O Thea, your love upholds me.

Your hands weave justice
and your voice sings truth;
 your love endures through every age.

U

My heart stands in awe of your wisdom,
 for it is my great love.

Great peace have they who love your wisdom;
 for no stumbling block is too great for them.

I soak in the balm of your presence, O Thea;
 I keep steady on your path.

I keep your wisdom close to my heart,
 and love you deeply.

Twenty-sixth Day: Evening Prayer

V

Let my creativity bear fruit before you, O Thea;
 stoke the fire of my imagination
 according to your wisdom.

My lips and hands and feet, indeed my whole body,
shall pour forth your praise
  as you teach me your ways.

I long for you, O Thea;
  our collaborative creativity is my delight.

W

Happy is she whose path is playful,
  who journeys in your imaginative ways, O Thea!

She spins and jumps,
she stomps and shouts,
  she tastes and smells and beholds with holy intention.

And when she sees another on the path,
she invites her into the dance
  for she seeks to meet you at every opportunity, O Thea.

X

You are my refuge and courage;
  my hope is in your Sacred Body.

Even when words fail and color dulls,
even when familiar fragrance fades and food is scarce,
  you are my faithful companion.

When those around me threaten to douse my sacred fire,
you invite me to let them go in a resounding yes
  to that which seeks to be tended within me.

And when that sacred fire crackles and glows once more,
  I shall teach others to tend their own bright fire,
    feeding, guarding, and sharing their light and warmth for all.

Y

I meditate on your wisdom
as I bear the fruit of creativity,
  and in your wisdom I take great comfort.

In the silence, and amidst joyful singing;
Alone, and amidst the many;
When my table is barren, and when my cup overflows:
  You are open to my presence.

Z

Let my creativity bear fruit before you, O Thea;
  stoke the fire of my imagination
  according to your wisdom.

Your hands weave justice
and your voice sings truth;
  your love endures through every age.

Let me ever remember, O Thea,
  that your hands are my hands
  and your voice is my voice.

Twenty-seventh Day: Morning Prayer

Psalm 120

Keep me, O Thea, from fostering lying lips
  and let not those around me give in to deceit.

Too long have I struggled toward the way of truth
  in the presence of those who love lies.

Show me your path of truth and justice, O Thea,
  and I shall invite others to journey it with me.

Psalm 121

I lift up my eyes to the hills;
  from where is my help to come?

My help comes from Thea,
  the author of all the universe.

She will keep me from stumbling;
  she will not let me fall asleep
  in the midst of danger.

Behold, she who keeps watch over me
  will stay by my side,

So that the sun will not strike me by day,
  nor the moon by night.

Thea will guide me away
from the path of harm;
  it is she who will show me to safety.

Thea will watch over my going out
and my coming in,
  from this day on until the end of my days.

Psalm 122

I was glad when they said to me,
  "Let us honor Thea among us."

We journey with you, O Thea,
  and we are part of you, O Sacred Body.

May we each pray for the peace of creation:
  "May all creatures love and honor one another.

As for me, O Sacred Body of Thea,
  I will seek to do you good."

Psalm 123

You open our hearts, O Thea;
  you open the hearts of those
  who are your Sacred Body.

We look to you, O Thea,
  discovering you in all your creatures.

Touch us with your love, O Thea,
  that we may touch wounded hearts,

Salve the eyes of those
  blind to the needs of their neighbors;

Mend the ears of those
  deaf to the cry of the poor;

And heal those who,
  through their own healing,
  will heal others.

Psalm 124

If Thea had not been with us,
  let the oppressed now say;

If Thea had not been with us,
  when our oppressors rose up against us;

Then they would have swallowed us up alive
  in their hatred toward us;

Then the waters would have overwhelmed us
  and the torrent gone right over us.

Blessed be Thea!
  she has not given us over to be a prey for their teeth.

We have escaped like a bird from the snare of the fowler;
  the snare is broken, and we have escaped.

Our help is in Thea,
   the author of all the universe.

Psalm 125

Thea's Sacred Body is like a mountain,
   which does not topple,
   but resists what would destroy it.

The scepter of self-interest shall not sway the just,
   for the just shall in all things
   act for the common good.

As for those who turn to unjust ways,
Thea will transform them,
   and peace shall prevail
   throughout her Sacred Body.

Twenty-seventh Day: Evening Prayer

Psalm 126

When Thea restored the lost,
   they were like those who dream;

Their mouths filled with laughter,
   and their tongues shouted for joy.

Those who once sowed with tears
   now reap with songs of joy.

Those who went out weeping,
carrying the seed,
   now come rejoicing,
   shouldering their sheaves.

Psalm 127

Unless you, O Thea, inspire the dwelling-place,
   her labor is in vain who builds it.

Unless you, O Thea, whisper the words,
   her labor is in vain who crafts the story.

It is in vain to rise so early
and go to bed so late;
   vain too, to eat the bread of toil
   without your guidance, O holy muse;

For it is you, O Thea, who gift your beloved
   with her holy, inimitable fire.

Psalm 128

Happy are you who behold Thea
   and journey in her ways!

You shall taste the fruit of your labor;
   happiness shall be yours.

May Thea bless you,
   and may your holy fire burn brightly
   all the days of your life.

Psalm 129

"Greatly has she oppressed me,"
   let me now say;

"Greatly has she oppressed me,
   but she has not prevailed against me."

For you, O Thea,
   have humbled the one who acted with cruelty.

She has been brought down
from her throne of might,
  she who embraced injustice.

Let her power be like grass upon the housetops,
  which withers before it can be plucked;

Which does not fill the hand of the reaper,
  nor the bosom of her who binds the sheaves.

In her desolation,
may her stony heart break open,
  that she may be touched by your wisdom.

Then may she join me
in claiming your wisdom's power:
  the power to feed, to forgive,
  to heal, to create, and to love.

Psalm 130

Out of the depths I call to you, O Thea;
  O Thea, hear my voice!

My flesh waits for you
  more than watchwomen for the morning.

All creation waits for you, O Thea,
  seeking the revelation of your love amid chaos.

Out of the depths we call to you, O Thea;
  O Thea, hear our cry!

Psalm 131

O Thea, I relinquish my busyness
  and every distracted glance.

For this moment,
I step away from great matters,
   from those challenges
   that stoke the fire within me.

Instead, I curl up in your arms
and grow quiet as a contented child,
   suckling sweet milk from your breast
   till I hunger no more.

Twenty-eighth Day: Morning Prayer

Psalm 132

O Thea, remember my foremothers,
   and all the hardships they endured;

How they swore an oath to you
   and vowed a solemn vow:

"I will not come under the roof of my house,
   nor climb up into my bed;

I will not allow my eyes to sleep,
   nor let my eyelids slumber;

Until I have honored Thea,
   the Mystery who dwells within me."

For you brought creation into being;
   you desire to dwell within and through your creatures:

"Creation shall be my Sacred Body forever;
   through creation I will move and bless,
   and I will delight in all my creatures.

I will clothe my priestesses with love,
   and all my creatures will rejoice and sing."

Psalm 133

Oh, how good and pleasant it is,
   when sisters live together in unity!

It is like fine oil upon a woman's head,
   that runs down upon her skin,
   and down the collar of her robe.

It is like the morning dew
   that swells upon the hills.

For it is in this unity
that Thea has ordained her blessing:
   love forevermore.

Psalm 134

Behold Thea,
   you who are her living icon.

Lift up your hands and bless creation;
   and may Thea, whose Sacred Body is creation,
   bless you.

Psalm 135

Sing to Thea, for she is wisdom's source;
   sing to her, for she is lovely.

Thea creates what delights her,
among the stars and throughout the earth,
   in the seas and all the deeps.

Thea loves her Sacred Body
   and shows compassion in every corner.

Blessed be Thea,
   whose Sacred Body is creation.
   Hallelujah!

Psalm 136

Give thanks to Thea,
  for her love is for all.

She works small and great wonders alike,
  for her love is for all;

She cast the celestial skies,
  for her love is for all;

She spread out the earth among the waters,
  for her love is for all;

She created the great lights,
  for her love is for all;

The sun to preside over the day,
  for her love is for all;

The moon and the stars to officiate the night,
  for her love is for all.

She remembers us in our darkest hour,
  for her love is for all;

And delivers us from all fear,
  for her love is for all;

She gives food to all who hunger,
  for her love is for all.

Let us give thanks to Thea,
  for her love is for all.

Psalm 137

By the waters of this foreign land we sit down and weep,
  when we remember you, O home of our hearts.

As for our instruments, we hang them up
    on the trees in the midst of this strange land.

Those who took us captive ask us for a song,
and our oppressors call for mirth:
    "Sing us one of your songs."

But how can we sing a song of joy
    while we dwell in captivity?

If I forget you, O home of my heart,
    let my hands forget their skill.

Let my tongue be muted,
if I do not remember you, my dear home,
    O blessed place where I once and may yet dwell free.

Psalm 138

I will give thanks to you, O Thea, with my whole heart;
    in the midst of creation, I will sing songs of you.

I will bow low in your presence,
    revering your Sacred Body.

When I call, you answer;
    you increase my strength within me.

Even when I journey through troubles,
    you give me courage.

You reveal your purpose for me piecemeal,
    and ever do I seek it;

O Thea, your love impels me to live as you do,
    and no desire is more precious to me.

Twenty-ninth Day: Morning Prayer

Psalm 139

O Thea, you know me;
  you know my resting and my rising;
  you discern the pattern of my thoughts.

You trace my journeys and my resting-places
  and are familiar with all my ways.

Indeed, there is not a word on my lips
  that you, O Thea, do not know.

You journey behind, before, and beside me,
  you impart your blessing
  with the touch of your hands.

Where can I go then from your love?
  where can I flee from your presence?

If I climb to the heavens, you are there;
  if I make the grave my bed, you are there also.

If I take the wings of the morning
  and fly to a place no one has ever known,

Even there you will accompany me
  and your hands hold mine in blessing.

If I say, "Surely the darkness will hide me,
  and the light around me turn to night,"

Darkness is not dark to you;
the night is as bright as the day;
  darkness and light to you are both alike.

For you yourself created my inmost parts;
  you knit me together in my mother's womb.

I will thank you because I am marvelously made;
  all your works are wonders to behold.

My body was not hidden from you,
   while I was being made in secret
   and woven in the depths.

Your eyes beheld my limbs,
yet unfinished in the womb;
   as they were fashioned day by day.

How deep I find your thoughts, O Thea!
   how great is the sum of them!

If I were to count them,
they would be more in number than the sand;
   to count them all,
   my life span would need to be like yours.

O Thea, you know my heart and you love me;
   lead me in your wisdom's way.

Psalm 140

Deliver the oppressed, O Thea,
   from the powerful ones who foster chaos
   and stir up strife all day long.

They sharpen their tongues like serpents;
   adder's poison is under their lips.

Grant us, O Thea, the wisdom and the courage
to unseat leaders who commit atrocities;
   help us protect one another from their violence.

For wicked leaders hide snares for us
and stretch out a net of ropes;
   they set traps for us along the path.

Hear us, O Thea;
   listen to our prayer.

Maintain the cause of the poor,
   and render justice to the needy;
   for you are our strength, O Thea.

Twenty-ninth Day: Evening Prayer

Psalm 141

O Thea, I call to you;
　　hear my whisper and my song.

Let my prayer arise like incense in your sight
　　as I lift my hands in an evening offering.

I keep watch over my mouth, O Thea,
　　and guard the door of my lips.

Let me not be swayed by those who do harm,
　　nor let me make merry at their table
　　while those outside go hungry.

Protect me from the self-interest that would ensnare me
　　and from the trap of greed that lures me.

My eyes turn to you, O Thea;
　　guide me on your path.

Psalm 142

O Thea, you know my path;
　　you see the trap that awaits me.

I look around and find no inspiration;
　　I have no place to call my own,
　　and my time is claimed by everyone but me.

But I cry out to you, O Thea;
　　I say, "You are my refuge, my creative haven."

Save me from the crowdedness
that would wither my creativity
　　and swallow me up.

Bring me out of this captivity, O Thea,
　　that I may create once more.

Psalm 143

O Thea, hear my voice;
  be my help, for I am utterly alone.

My enemy has sought my life;
she has crushed me to the ground;
  she has forced me to dwell in dark places
  like those who are long dead.

My flesh wanes and withers;
  my heart despairs.

I spread out my hands to you;
  my flesh gasps for you like a thirsty land.

Let me wake to your loving-kindness in the morning,
  for you alone do I trust;

Revive me, O Thea;
  rescue me from that which would destroy me.

Thirtieth Day: Morning Prayer

Psalm 144

O Thea, we sing to you a new song;
  we play to you on well-loved instruments.

For our daughters are growing up like cedars
  strong, great, and unbreaking.

Our gardens are full of thriving plants
  whose seeds we planted ourselves.

There is no more breaching of our boundaries,
  no exile from the land we call home.

We give thanks to you, O Thea,
  for you have shown us the way of strength and vitality.

May we bless your Sacred Body
for all the rest of our days!
   Hallelujah!

Psalm 145

Every day I will bless you, O Thea,
   and journey at your side.

The eyes of all wait upon you, O Thea,
   and you give them their food in due season.

I shall hand down the stories of your kindness;
   and sing of your loving deeds.

You uphold those who stumble;
   you lift up those who are bent low.

You open wide your hand
   and reveal your great abundance.

You are near to those who call upon you,
   nearer than they can even imagine.

You fulfill the deepest desires of your Sacred Body;
   you take up your true call.

My mouth shall sing to you, O Thea;
   may your Sacred Body bear blessing upon blessing.

Psalm 146

I love you, O Thea, my flesh and my song!
   I will rejoice in you as long as I live.

For you are the seas and the stars
   the universe and all that lay beyond it.

You seek justice for those who dwell in oppression
   and food for those who hunger.

You set prisoners free;
You open the eyes of the blind;
  You lift up those bent low with weariness.

You welcome the stranger;
  you protect the vulnerable.

You shall dwell in and among us forever.
  Hallelujah!

Thirtieth Day: Evening Prayer

Psalm 147

How good it is to sing to Thea!
  how sweet it is to honor her with a song!

For Thea builds up creation, her Sacred Body;
  she gathers all her creatures to herself,
  loving into being their tremendous diversity.

She heals the brokenhearted
  and binds up their wounds.

She counts every star and grain of sand
and everything beyond and between
  calling each one by name.

She provides food for flocks, herds, and peoples,
  and for the young ravens when they cry.

She strengthens our boundaries and widens our doors;
  she blesses our children with all her heart.

She establishes peace among us;
  she satisfies us with finest wheat.

She sends forth her word and it melts icy hearts;
  she breathes, and the once frozen waters flow.

Psalm 148

Praise Thea, O creation;
 praise her in the heights and depths.

Praise her, sun and moon;
 praise her, all you glittering stars.

Praise Thea from the earth,
 you sea-creatures and all deeps;

Fire and hail, snow and fog,
 tempestuous wind;

Mountains and all hills,
 fruit trees and tall cedars;

Wild beasts and cattle,
 creeping things and winged birds;

Persons of every body, heritage, and worldview,
 artists and warriors,
 inspirers and inspired together.

Let us all praise Thea,
 for her splendor is who we are, her Sacred Body.
 Hallelujah!

Psalm 149

Sing a new song in the great gathering;
 sing as one Sacred Body!

Let us rejoice in Thea our author;
 let us be joyful in who we are.

Let us praise her in the dance;
 let us sing, playing the strings and the drum.

For Thea takes pleasure in each of us
 and surrounds us with the beauty of her love.

Let the praises of Thea's Sacred Body
rise in our throats.
    Hallelujah!

Psalm 150

Hallelujah!
Praise Thea's Sacred Body;
    praise the loving power of her imagination.

Praise her with the blast of the horn;
    praise her with the strings and the drum.

Praise her with the ecstasy of the dance;
    praise her with the roar of creative fire.

Praise her with resounding cymbals;
    praise her with thundering bodies.

Let Thea's Sacred Body
sound her great and holy voice!
    Hallelujah!